I0519311

No Ocean Spit Me Out

No Ocean Spit Me Out

Gabby Gilliam

No Ocean Spit Me Out

Copyright ©2024 Gabby Gilliam.

Published by Old Scratch Press, an imprint of Current Words Publishing, LLC.
All rights reserved. No part of this publication may be reproduced, distributed, or transmitted in any form by any means, including photocopying, recording, or other electronic methods without the prior written permission of the author, except in the case of brief quotations embodied in reviews and certain other noncommercial uses permitted by copyright law.
For permission requests, contact the publisher.

ISBN:978-1-957224-32-9 (print)
ISBN: 978-1-957224-33-6 (epub)

Printed in the United States of America.

FIND US AT

oldscratchpress.com
currentwords.com

Contents

11   Visiting the North Country
12   Going Home
13   Babka
14   Just the Once
16   Dishonest Day's Work
17   Grandpa Russ
18   Blackberry Wine
19   Filling the Table
20   You Were
21   Going to Seed
22   Raised Catholic
23   First Communion
24   I Don't Like Sundays
25   No Ocean Spit Me Out
26   A Sliver of Sky
27   Don't Tell Me It Will Pass
28   Transcendence of Stars
29   My Apologies, Dad
30   Wearing Your Absence
31   Empty Nest
32   Staying With My Mother
33   Is My Tree Dying or Dead?
34   She Promised Us Each a Quilt
35   This I Know
36   Not All Venom Will Kill You
37   Act of Contrition
38   Self-Portrait
39   Running Free
40   My Morning Run Grants Absolution in Every Breath
41   I Will Celebrate Each Revolution
43   Acknowledgements
44   Bio

for Dad

No Ocean Spit Me Out

Visiting the North Country

I dream of the Adirondacks.
Rubbery brine of cheese
curd chewed on the shores
of Stillwater Reservoir.
Croghan bologna on crackers.
The unexpected tug
on my line. Yellow perch
slick as memory. Caught and released.

Going Home

Porch lights flicker in the trees
like fireflies under the darkened sky
winking in and out of existence
the way memories do
when you're not remembering them.

I wander through the rooms
that were once so familiar
and the dining room
is in the old carport

and a sewing machine
has replaced my bed and my closet
is filled with clothes
that don't belong to me.

It hurts to acknowledge
that this place is no longer mine
when my feet helped scuff
these hardwood floors and the walls
have witnessed my weeping.

And I wonder how long my laughter
will echo in these halls

when I became a stranger
in this place that is no longer home.

Babka

Her kitchen smelled of peppers
and Polish sausage. She stood over
the stove, cooking an epic feast
just to feed the four of us.

Her rings glittered, reflecting the light
from over the stove, pressed slacks and silk
blouse visible even if her clothes were masked
by an apron. Hair meticulously curled

sat perfectly atop her head
and the heels of her polished shoes
clicked as she bustled about
on the spotless linoleum floor.

Now that time has caught her, she no longer
makes kielbasa or sauerkraut. Her hands
are idle and bare. Her knuckles, bent
and disfigured, she can no longer wear her rings.

Her face protected from the sun by a floppy
straw hat, with a pink ribbon that flutters
gracefully when caught by the wind. She kneels
in her garden, her dirty calloused hands easing
a velvety purple iris into the ground.

Just the Once

My grandmother's tree grew
the tiniest apples
covered the driveway
and part of the front walk
with diminutive fruit
perfectly sized
for my groping fingers

and I would ask my mother
to let me eat one
every time we went to visit.

"You won't like it,"
my mother would say

which only made me want
to try them even more.

The day came
when I found myself
in the soft grass
of my grandmother's yard
with no mother to deny me.

I plucked an apple
so petite, red skin flecked
with patches of green
brought it to expectant lips
took that first savory bite

and spit it into the grass
chucking the rest of the apple
across the driveway
for the birds to eat.

My grandmother chuckled
when I said her apples
were gross—she agreed
told me she didn't care
for crabapples either.

Dishonest Day's Work

The summer I pack vodka in my suitcase
for a month at Grandma and Grandpa's
my grandfather decides my sister and I
are responsible enough to run the vegetable stand.

We sell deep green zucchinis as big as my thigh
and unshucked ears of corn by the baker's dozen,
though Grandpa calls it a farmer's dozen, and the stand
smells fresh, the corn silky green as new spring grass.

I sneak worn green bills into my pockets
swear my little sister to secrecy with promises
of edible gifts using my ill-gained profits.
But my mother finds the stash of ones

when someone snitches about the vodka.
She forces me to return each tainted
dollar to my grandfather who masks
his disappointment that all I can sow is mistrust.

Grandpa Russ

He rose with the sun, and dinner called him
home— thin, gray hair sprinkled

with bits of hay and dirt, favorite pipe
threatening to fall through threadbare pocket—

faded red suspenders resting limply
on the thighs of dark olive pants,

stained and covered in dirt—coarse hands
blackened from hours spent with crops.

He served us sweet corn from a field
that he harvested with his own hands;

fried zucchini, pattypan and yellow squash
grown in the soil of his backyard garden.

There was fresh milk coaxed into a milk can
by his hands, and brought home along

with the smell of the cows,
and the hay, and the mud on his boots,

which he placed outside the front door
so he wouldn't track work into the house.

Blackberry Wine

You stumble through the woods
crimson-fingered, clothes stained,
covered entirely in dark juice.

Your hands are scratched
and bleeding, both blood
and juice running toward elbows.

You tenderly pick one more
plump, ripe blackberry,
place it in the bowl pinned
between your hip and elbow.

When you get home, you pour
the berries into the tub,
brutally mash them into little bits,
take all the juice from them you can.

I've seen a wine-making gone bad
all over the walls and floor
of your small bathroom; the bathtub
littered with particles of stem and berries.

I've tasted the results
of a wine-making
that hasn't gone bad,
felt it burn all the way down.

The glass jug was heavy
and smelled nothing like berries,
tasted nothing like berries.

My throat burned for hours.

Filling the Table

My dad and his brothers
grew up in the North Country

shooting rabbits so they could eat,
picking wild berries to keep

their bellies from cramping.
When you are poor enough

you learn how to shoot so you
won't know how it feels to starve.

Dad taught us to fish and hunt
to filet catfish and dress deer

to fill our plates and freezer.
We planted a backyard garden

to curtail the grocery bill;
sun-warmed peas sweet on the tongue

tomatoes canned for the winter,
cucumbers pickled and flavored

with dill or brown sugar and celery seed.
We foraged wild strawberries

and blackberries from the field
across the driveway

both bowls and bellies filled
with the sweetness of summer sun.

You Were

Croghan bologna and New York cheddar
on crackers for dinner

Milwaukee's Best Ice in a coozie
with another cold one on deck
usually tucked into your back pocket

threadbare flannel and Wrangler jeans

two packs of Winchesters a day
gasped into cancerous lungs

venison burgers over beef

the soft sound of horseshoes
burrowing into sand

rhythmless shuffling on the dance floor
in a gray suit and dirty tennis shoes

breakfast for dinner

answering the phone with a color
instead of a salutation

a voice on the wind calling
to my open window and taillights
"It was real good seeing you."

Going to Seed

This overgrown field
smells like autumn afternoons,
homework forgotten.

High golden grass drinks waning sunlight. Rotten crabapples
crushed underfoot. The crunch of gravel beneath your tires as you
snake down the long driveway, elbow propped out of your open
window.

Golden field stretches
Shadows lengthening with time.
Gradual forest.

Your truck idle in the driveway. Your ashes in a box on a shelf
where the wind can't rustle your branches. And I stand alone in this
new field a hundred miles from that old wildness. I crack a milk-
weed pod with my hands. Free the seeds to find their own fertile
earth.

Raised Catholic

The roots of your faith were buried
deep—hidden beneath stubble
and calloused skin as you shifted

weight from foot to foot,
back pressed against the wall

—a piece of flesh on your tongue
and then straight to the car.

The hymns didn't hum in your chest.
The prayers rarely crossed your lips
but you held up that wall every Sunday

and I wonder if the altar boys recited
the routine of your memory

if every congregation
of sin smells the same

if you confessed while waiting
in the parking lot—found
absolution in the open air.

First Communion

I expected a burst
of happiness on my tongue,
the tingle of salvation
as transubstantiated flesh
tickled its way down my throat

but only found the whisper
of crisp robes and a stale wafer,
which melted into paste
and tasted nothing like peace.

I would have coughed to clear it
from my mouth or spit it out
if Jesus hadn't been watching
from his crucifix, open wounds
oozing with forgiveness.

I Don't Like Sundays

As the flesh melted
from your bones,
stray cash disappeared.

It was little things at first;
a missing piggy bank,
bills missing from purses.

One Sunday we came home
from church to find you had
raided the house for valuables.

I listened to our parents
fight about whether
they would press charges.

We staked your boyfriend's place out
like we were on a cop show instead
of a broken family dressed in our Sunday best.

When you went into his house
we drove to the corner store,
used a payphone to call the police.

Did the boyfriend ever come visit
you in jail or rehab? We did—
driving out to sit through

family therapy sessions
every Sunday, like healing you
was our new homily.

No Ocean Spit Me Out

You were born in a burst
of sea foam, a pearl
rising from sand,
salt-kissed and beautiful.

I was born in upstate New York
—no further North than that—
snow-kissed fingers and toes
never able to get warm.

Your father wielded lightning,
his fury immortal.

My father wielded weed-whackers
and grill tongs—his anger
dull sparks that failed to ignite,
his love enduring beyond
the limits of his mortality.

Did Zeus ever tuck you in?
Ignore the flashlight clutched
beneath your sheets so you
could read after lights out?

Did he sing old gospel songs
into the darkness while
your eyelids grew heavy?

Or did he only turn maidens into cows?

A Sliver of Sky

You wore this faded
plaid like a second skin
carried it into the wilderness
to track deer in gauzy pre-dawn light.

Threadbare pocket protected
your unsmoked Winchesters.
Flannel absorbed sweet vapor of filtered cigars
burnt tobacco staining fingers, teeth, and lungs.

You folded these sleeves over your tumors
pressed them close to your infested chest.
We wrapped your body in this shirt's sister
—a different plaid to mingle with your ash.

But this one I pull close
let it banish Spring's lingering chill.

Don't Tell Me It Will Pass

My molars ache
from clenching my jaw,
grinding bone against bone
while I chew this fresh grief.

They will lay your bones
in North Carolina earth
two days from now.

I air out my funeral dress
to rid it of the stale
scent of the last death
still clinging to its hem,
ready to pack these feelings
into my overnight bag.

I spit shards of shattered tooth
onto the shoulder as I drive.

Transcendence of Stars

after Hollis Sigler

My mother would
love this painting

the gradual
transmutation
from flesh to wing

figures cocooned
in a column of light

illumination a mercy
that caressed
their upturned faces.

How she has searched
for a bloom of feathers

to feel the rush of salvation
whisper across her lips.

My Apologies, Dad

The marbled stumps of graves
poke out of overgrown grass,
an army of gray thumbs
in perfect steadfast formation.

We didn't open the windows
or stop the clocks when you died.

I hold my breath until
we pass the final row
to avoid catching my death
or angering an envious spirit
with my functional lungs
my beating heart
my tightly pressed lips.

I just learned you're supposed
to tuck thumbs into fists while passing
a cemetery to protect your parents.

I never knew. So many
ways I failed to protect you.

Wearing Your Absence

In the thin gray light of early morning
I fail to notice the silvery threads
until my face severs them. Sticky
strings cling to my cheeks. I clutch
at web with frenzied fingers, but like
your death, no matter how I pick
I feel their trespass crawling with
the potential threat of piercing fangs
defending a sundered home and my terror
keeps me trapped and smothered, pinned
by panic, limbs twitching to set me free.

Empty Nest

Here where she once
kept the home's fire
burning brightly

hearth now filled with ash
soot-stained floorboards
worn thin by our footfalls

shingles warped and wind-torn
siding cracked and algae-slick,
empty beds haunt silent rooms.

An old woman lurks in shadow,
wraps herself in solitude
indifferent to the dark.

Staying With My Mother

I climb into routine
like it's a lost cardigan
recovered from a closet corner.

I remember how it used to feel
but the weight on my shoulders
is no longer familiar.

Is My Tree Dying or Dead?

I try to channel the memory
of my ancestors, search
with stunted roots in soil
too virgin to be fertile.

I cannot drink their wisdom,
scrape only the surface
of their histories while time
burns our tenuous connection

severs me from the ancient
power of past generations.

A lone branch
on a barren family tree.

She Promised Us Each a Quilt

The pain in my mother's wrists
doesn't discriminate—throbbing
within taut tissue as she pulls
another stretch of quilt across
the sewing machine's arm.

Since my father's funeral
she has attacked her fabric stash,
a torrent of stitches to distract her
from his absence. She lets his loss
pool in the shadows at her feet,
nudges it aside to press the pedal
as she feeds pinned squares
to the needle. When the sun dips
below the treeline, she leans
over to turn on the light.

This I Know

The soil of upstate New York
is nourished with my ancestors,
bone and sinew broken down,
persisting in roots and branches.

That I shed blood and tissue
to create a copy of myself,
incubated him in a public library,
fed him books and songs so he sings
Hamilton to his graphic novels.

This fleshy husk is finite;
HydrogenCarbonOxygenNitrogen
a kindness the universe lends us
that will return to soil and stardust.

Gabby Gilliam

Not All Venom Will Kill You

I carry my ancestors close
to my skin, thrumming

through capillaries, clogging
my pores, phantom eyes

tracking every misstep,
their silent judgment captured

in disapproving stares;
our joint history a chronicle

of my mistakes, each
memory a scorpion sting.

Act of Contrition

I bruised my knees
begging for your forgiveness

counted plastic beads
as I repeated the prayers

a priest's prescription for penance
of my childhood sins.

How many Hail Marys would I get now that I use
my knees for a different type of service?

Can our Lady of Peace
offer an olive branch

or is my mouth too soiled
to hold absolution on my tongue?

Self-portrait

I am plates picked clean
except for the last bite,
tepid tea on tables,
ink-stained fingers and echoes
of the North Country.
I am a farmer without roots
or soil—dirty fingernails
but no harvest—honed pocketknife
fierce edge unwielded, still
anticipating its first cut.

Running Free

I am wild strawberries,
explosion of juice on tongue

barefoot on gravel,
feet calloused and sure

sap-stained palms and racing
to the highest limb

ghost in the graveyard beneath
a full summer moon

the lemony tartness
of crabgrass blossoms

syrupy sweetness
licked from honeysuckle

the echo of summer freedom
still ringing in my bones.

Gabby Gilliam

My Morning Run Grants Absolution in Every Breath

I clutch at laces like rosary beads,
taut knots instead of Hail Marys

let my soles whisper
penance to the pavement

while crisp autumn sunlight
presses deliverance into my skin.

I Will Celebrate Each Revolution

I could devour this
morning—belly full
of dew-kissed grass

birdsong nesting
gently in my throat

my breath fragrant
with possibility

taste of dawn brilliant
on my tongue.

Acknowledgements

This book likely wouldn't have happened without the support of my first creative writing teachers in high school. Miss Sydnor and Miss Peters read all of my emo teen-angsty poems and offered nothing but encouragement. I might have put my pen away forever after graduation if they hadn't supported those early endeavors. Both of you will forever have my gratitude.

I would like to thank the poetry group at Quince Orchard Library who helped workshop the earliest drafts of some of these poems. A special thanks to Eve Burton who facilitates those poetry groups and provided prompts that gave birth to the poems I workshopped with those poets. Also to Geoff and the poets in the diVERSES Chapbook Chamber who gave thorough feedback on a rough draft of this chapbook.

To Kim Malinowski for providing prompts made of magnetic words and for quick responses to emails of poetry drafts.

I'd also like to thank Dianne Pearce and David Yurkovich who decided to launch the Old Scratch Short Form Collective and Old Scratch Press. Without them and the other founding members of Old Scratch Press, this collection wouldn't be here. To Nadja and Anthony, thank you so much for proofreading. Your feedback was incredibly helpful, and this book wouldn't exist in its current state without you.

To my husband and son who gave me time and space to write and listened to drafts of these poems when I needed to hear them out loud. You guys are the best.

Many thanks to the editors of the following journals in which these poems first appeared, some in slightly different forms.

Anti-Heroin Chic, "I Don't Like Sundays"
The Chesapeake Reader: "Babka"

Acknowledgements

Full House, *Tarot 3*, "Wearing Your Absence"
Holiday Cafe: "Is My Tree Dying or Dead?"
Instant Noodles: "Going Home"
Isele, "Filling the Table"
Lothlorien Poetry Journal: "Act of Contrition"
The Poetry Box, "My Apologies, Dad"
Pure Slush *Vol. 23, Cow*: "Grandpa Russ"
Silver Birch Press, "She Promised Us Each a Quilt"
Superfroot: "Just the Once"
Tofu Ink Arts Press: "No Ocean Spit Me Out" and "Raised Catholic"
Vermillion: "A Sliver of Sky"
White Stag Publishing, *SPIRIT*: "Transcendence of Stars"

About the Author

GABBY GILLIAM is a writer, an aspiring teacher, and a mom. She was born in upstate New York, but moved to Virginia when she was four. The rural landscapes of her youth make frequent appearances in her poems. She now lives in the D.C. metro area with her husband and son.

Gabby is the author of two novellas: *Drumming for the Dead: Trouble in Tomsk* and *Drumming for the Dead: Chasing a Cure*, both published by Black Hare Press. Her poetry has appeared in *One Art, Anti-Heroin Chic, Plant-Human Quarterly, The Ekphrastic Review, Vermillion, Deep Overstock, Spank the Carp*, and others. Her fiction has appeared in *Grim & Gilded* and multiple anthologies. *No Ocean Spit Me Out* is her first chapbook.

More at gabbygilliam.com

Founded in 2023, Old Scratch Press is a
cooperative of poets and short-form authors
who have come together to promote the
publication and appreciation of poetry
and short-form writing.
Robert Fleming's **white noir** is the second book
from this endeavor. We hope you've enjoyed it.

oldscratchpress.com

oldscratchpress.com

Devil's Party Press proudly presents an original short story collection by acclaimed author Virgina Watts.

ECHOES FROM THE HOCKER HOUSE

Best Indie Books of 2023 [KIRKUS]
2024 Grand Prize Short List [Eric Hoffer Book Awards]
WINNER: 2024 Feathered Quill Book Awards (BRONZE)
2023 National Book Award Nominee

"Entrancing, edgy, and melodramatic tales with a palpable bite."
KIRKUS

15 visceral tales | 194 unforgettable pages

Available at all major online retailers and better bookstores.

devilspartypress.com

virginiawatts.com

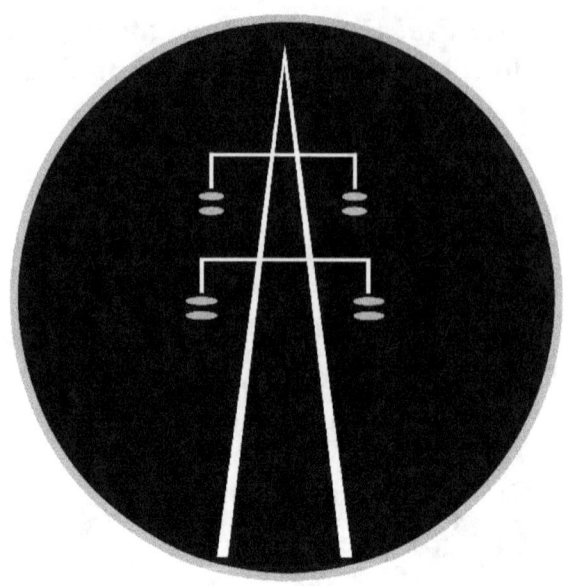

INTRODUCING CURRENT WORDS PUBLISHING

We're a multi-media book publisher offering a personalized approach to the publishing and marketing of your book.

We Provide:

Publishing Services
1:1 Coaching
Editing and Design
Audiobook Creation
Marketing Services
Vella to Book

Why authors choose us:

Personal engagement
40+ years of combined experience
Attentiveness to your needs
Top-quality editing, production, and design
Honesty and integrity

Learn more and take the first step toward publication excellence, by visiting us on the web.

currentwords.com

www.ingramcontent.com/pod-product-compliance
Lightning Source LLC
Chambersburg PA
CBHW070947120626
46546CB00004B/1601